Palgrave Golden Treasury of Love Poems

A Phoenix Paperback

Palgrave's Golden Treasury first published
by J. M. Dent in 1955

This abridged edition published in 1996 by Phoenix
a division of Orion Books Ltd
Orion House, 5 Upper St Martin's Lane, London WC2H 9EA

1 85799 555 4

Typeset at The Spartan Press Ltd,
Lymington, Hants
Printed in Great Britain by Clays Ltd, St Ives plc

CONTENTS

CHRISTOPHER MARLOWE
The Passionate Shepherd to His Love　1

WILLIAM SHAKESPEARE
'It was a lover and his lass'　2
A Consolation　3
True Love　4
Blind Love　4

SIR PHILIP SIDNEY
A Ditty　5

MICHAEL DRAYTON
Love's Farewell　6

COLONEL LOVELACE
To Lucasta, On Going To The Wars　7

BEN JONSON
To Celia　7

ROBERT HERRICK
To Anthea Who May Command Him Any Thing 8

ANON
'Love not me for comely grace' 9

SIR JOHN SUCKLING
Encouragements To A Lover 10

SIR GEORGE WITHER
The Manly Heart 11

ANON
Fair Helen 12

JOHN GAY
Black-Eyed Susan 14

HENRY CAREY
Sally In Our Alley 16

ROBERT BURNS
'Ye banks and braes o' bonnie Doon' 19
'O my Luve's like a red, red rose' 20
John Anderson 21

SAMUEL TAYLOR COLERIDGE
Love 21

LORD BYRON
All For Love   26
She walks in beauty, like the night   27
When we two parted   28
Elegy on Thyrza   29

WILLIAM WORDSWORTH
The Lost Love   32
Desideria   33

THOMAS CAMPBELL
Freedom And Love   33

PERCY BYSSHE SHELLEY
Love's Philosophy   35
The Flight Of Love   35

SIR WALTER SCOTT
Where Shall the Lover Rest   37
The Maid of Neidpath   39

JOHN KEATS
La Belle Dame Sans Merci   40

JAMES CLARENCE MANGAN
Dark Rosaleen   42

ELIZABETH BARRETT BROWNING
Sonnet From The Portuguese   46
The Ways of Love   46

LORD TENNYSON
The Lady of Shalott   47

EMILY BRONTË
Remembrance   54

DANTE GABRIEL ROSSETTI
Silent Noon   56

W. B. YEATS
'When you are old and gray and full of sleep'   56
Down By The Salley Gardens   57

CHRISTOPHER MARLOWE

The Passionate Shepherd to His Love

Come live with me and be my Love,
And we will all the pleasures prove
That hills and valleys, dale and field,
And all the craggy mountains yield.

There will we sit upon the rocks
And see the shepherds feed their flocks,
By shallow rivers, to whose falls
Melodious birds sing madrigals.

There will I make thee beds of roses
And a thousand fragrant posies,
A cap of flowers, and a kirtle
Embroider'd all with leaves of myrtle.

A gown made of the finest wool,
Which from our pretty lambs we pull,
Fair linéd slippers for the cold,
With buckles of the purest gold.

A belt of straw and ivy buds
With coral clasps and amber studs:

And if these pleasures may thee move,
Come live with me and be my Love.

Thy silver dishes for thy meat
As precious as the gods do eat,
Shall on an ivory table be
Prepared each day for thee and me.

The shepherd swains shall dance and sing
For thy delight each May-morning:
If these delights thy mind may move,
Then live with me and be my Love.

WILLIAM SHAKESPEARE

'It was a lover and his lass'

It was a lover and his lass
   With a hey and a ho, and a hey-nonino!
That o'er the green corn-field did pass
In the spring time, the only pretty ring time,
When birds do sing hey ding a ding:
   Sweet lovers love the Spring.

Between the acres of the rye
These pretty country folks would lie:
This carol they began that hour,
How that life was but a flower:

And therefore take the present time
    With a hey and a ho and a hey-nonino!
For love is crownéd with the prime
In the spring time, the only pretty ring time,
When birds do sing hey ding a ding:
    Sweet lovers love the Spring.

WILLIAM SHAKESPEARE

A Consolation

When in disgrace with fortune and men's eyes
I all alone beweep my outcast state,
And trouble deaf heaven with my bootless cries,
And look upon myself, and curse my fate;

Wishing me like to one more rich in hope,
Featured like him, like him with friends possest,
Desiring this man's art, and that man's scope,
With what I most enjoy contented least;

Yet in these thoughts myself almost despising,
Haply I think on Thee – and then my state,
Like to the lark at break of day arising
From sullen earth, sings hymns at heaven's gate;

For thy sweet love remember'd, such wealth brings
That then I scorn to change my state with kings.

WILLIAM SHAKESPEARE

True Love

Let me not to the marriage of true minds
Admit impediments. Love is not love
Which alters when it alteration finds,
Or bends with the remover to remove:—

O no! it is an ever-fixéd mark
That looks on tempests, and is never shaken;
It is the star to every wandering bark,
Whose worth's unknown, although his height be taken.

Love's not Time's fool, though rosy lips and cheeks
Within his bending sickle's compass come;
Love alters not with his brief hours and weeks,
But bears it out ev'n to the edge of doom:—

If this be error, and upon me proved,
I never writ, nor no man ever loved.

WILLIAM SHAKESPEARE

Blind Love

O me! what eyes hath love put in my head
Which have no correspondence with true sight:

Or if they have, where is my judgment fled
That censures falsely what they see aright?

If that be fair whereon my false eyes dote,
What means the world to say it is not so?
If it be not, then love doth well denote
Love's eye is not so true as all men's: No,

How can it? O how can love's eye be true,
That is so vex'd with watching and with tears?
No marvel then though I mistake my view:
The sun itself sees not till heaven clears.

O cunning Love! with tears thou keep'st me blind
Lest eyes well-seeing thy foul faults should find!

SIR PHILIP SIDNEY

A Ditty

My true-love hath my heart, and I have his,
By just exchange one for another given:
I hold his dear, and mine he cannot miss,
There never was a better bargain driven:
    My true-love hath my heart, and I have his.

His heart in me keeps him and me in one,
My heart in him his thoughts and senses guides:

He loves my heart, for once it was his own,
I cherish his because in me it bides:
  My true-love hath my heart, and I have his.

MICHAEL DRAYTON

Love's Farewell

Since there's no help, come let us kiss and part, –
Nay I have done, you get no more of me;
And I am glad, yea, glad with all my heart,
That thus so cleanly I myself can free;

Shake hands for ever, cancel all our vows,
And when we meet at any time again,
Be it not seen in either of our brows
That we one jot of former love retain.

Now at the last gasp of love's latest breath,
When his pulse failing, passion speechless lies,
When faith is kneeling by his bed of death,
And innocence is closing up his eyes,

– Now if thou would'st, when all have given him over,
From death to life thou might'st him yet recover!

To Lucasta, On Going To The Wars

Tell me not, Sweet, I am unkind
 That from the nunnery
Of thy chaste breast and quiet mind,
 To war and arms I fly.

True, a new mistress now I chase,
 The first foe in the field;
And with a stronger faith embrace
 A sword, a horse, a shield.

Yet this inconstancy is such
 As you too shall adore;
I could not love thee, Dear, so much,
 Loved I not Honour more.

To Celia

Drink to me only with thine eyes,
 And I will pledge with mine;
Or leave a kiss but in the cup
 And I'll not look for wine.
The thirst that from the soul doth rise

Doth ask a drink divine;
But might I of Jove's nectar sup,
    I would not change for thine.

I sent thee late a rosy wreath,
    Not so much honouring thee
As giving it a hope that there
    It could not wither'd be;
But thou thereon didst only breathe
    And sent'st it back to me;
Since when it grows, and smells, I swear,
    Not of itself but thee!

ROBERT HERRICK

To Anthea Who May Command Him Any Thing

Bid me to live, and I will live
    Thy Protestant to be:
Or bid me love, and I will give
    A loving heart to thee.

A heart as soft, a heart as kind,
    A heart as sound and free
As in the whole world thou canst find,
    That heart I'll give to thee.

Bid that heart stay, and it will stay,

To honour thy decree:
Or bid it languish quite away,
  And 't shall do so for thee.

Bid me to weep, and I will weep
  While I have eyes to see:
And having none, yet I will keep
  A heart to weep for thee.

Bid me despair, and I'll despair,
  Under that cypress tree:
Or bid me die, and I will dare
  E'en Death, to die for thee.

Thou art my life, my love, my heart,
  The very eyes of me,
And hast command of every part,
  To live and die for thee.

ANON

'Love not me for comely grace'

Love not me for comely grace,
For my pleasing eye or face,
Nor for any outward part,
No, nor for my constant heart, —
  For those may fail, or turn to ill,

So thou and I shall sever:
Keep therefore a true woman's eye,
And love me still, but know not why —
So hast thou the same reason still
To doat upon me ever!

SIR JOHN SUCKLING

Encouragements To A Lover

Why so pale and wan, fond lover?
Prythee, why so pale?
Will, if looking well can't move her,
Looking ill prevail?
Prythee, why so pale?

Why so dull and mute, young sinner?
Prythee, why so mute?
Will, when speaking well can't win her,
Saying nothing do't?
Prythee, why so mute?

Quit, quit, for shame! this will not move,
This cannot take her;
If of herself she will not love,
Nothing can make her:
The D—l take her!

SIR GEORGE WITHER

The Manly Heart

Shall I, wasting in despair,
Die because a woman's fair?
Or my cheeks make pale with care
'Cause another's rosy are?
Be she fairer than the day
Or the flowery meads in May –
    If she be not so to me
    What care I how fair she be?

Shall my foolish heart be pined
'Cause I see a woman kind;
Or a well disposéd nature
Joinéd with a lovely feature?
Be she meeker, kinder, than
Turtle-dove or pelican,
    If she be not so to me
    What care I how kind she be?

Shall a woman's virtues move
Me to perish for her love?
Or her merits' value known
Make me quite forget mine own?
Be she with that goodness blest
Which may gain her name of Best;
    If she seem not such to me,

What care I how good she be?

'Cause her fortune seems too high,
Shall I play the fool and die?
Those that bear a noble mind
Where they want of riches find,
Think what with them they would do
Who without them dare to woo;
    And unless that mind I see,
    What care I how great she be?

Great or good, or kind or fair,
I will ne'er the more despair;
If she love me, this believe,
I will die ere she shall grieve;
If she slight me when I woo,
I can scorn and let her go;
    For if she be not for me,
    What care I for whom she be?

ANON

Fair Helen

I wish I were where Helen lies;
Night and day on me she cries;
O that I were where Helen lies
    On fair Kirconnell lea!

Curst be the heart that thought the thought,
And curst the hand that fired the shot,
When in my arms burd Helen dropt,
    And died to succour me!

O think na but my heart was sair
When my Love dropt down and spak nae mair!
I laid her down wi' meikle care
    On fair Kirconnell lea.

As I went down the water-side,
None but my foe to be my guide,
None but my foe to be my guide,
    On fair Kirconnell lea;

I lighted down my sword to draw,
I hackéd him in pieces sma',
I hackéd him in pieces sma',
    For her sake that died for me.

O Helen fair, beyond comparc!
I'll make a garland of thy hair
Shall bind my heart for evermair
    Until the day I die.

O that I were where Helen lies!
Night and day on me she cries;
Out of my bed she bids me rise,
    Says, 'Haste and come to me!'

O Helen fair! O Helen chaste!
If I were with thee, I were blest,
Where thou lies low and takes thy rest
    On fair Kirconnell lea.

I wish my grave were growing green,
A winding-sheet drawn ower my een,
And I in Helen's arms lying,
    On fair Kirconnell lea.

I wish I were where Helen lies;
Night and day on me she cries;
And I am weary of the skies
    Since my Love died for me.

JOHN GAY

Black-Eyed Susan

All in the Downs the fleet was moor'd,
   The streamers waving in the wind,
When black-eyed Susan came aboard;
   'O! where shall I my true-love find?
Tell me, ye jovial sailors, tell me true
If my sweet William sails among the crew.'

William who high upon the yard
   Rock'd with the billow to and fro,

Soon as her well-known voice he heard
   He sigh'd, and cast his eyes below:
The cord slides swiftly through his glowing hands,
And quick as lightning on the deck he stands.

So the sweet lark, high poised in air,
   Shuts close his pinions to his breast
If chance his mate's shrill call he hear,
   And drops at once into her nest:—
The noblest captain in the British fleet
Might envy William's lip those kisses sweet.

'O Susan, Susan, lovely dear,
   My vows shall ever true remain;
Let me kiss off that falling tear;
   We only part to meet again.
Change as ye list, ye winds; my heart shall be
The faithful compass that still points to thee.

'Believe not what the landmen say
   Who tempt with doubts thy constant mind:
They'll tell thee, sailors, when away,
   In every port a mistress find:
Yes, yes, believe them when they tell thee so,
For Thou art present wheresoe'er I go.

'If to fair India's coast we sail,
   Thy eyes are seen in diamonds bright,

Thy breath is Afric's spicy gale,
  Thy skin is ivory so white.
Thus every beauteous object that I view
Wakes in my soul some charm of lovely Sue.

'Though battle call me from thy arms
  Let not my pretty Susan mourn;
Though cannons roar, yet safe from harms
  William shall to his Dear return.
Love turns aside the balls that round me fly,
Lest precious tears should drop from Susan's eye.'

The boatswain gave the dreadful word,
  The sails their swelling bosom spread,
No longer must she stay aboard;
  They kiss'd, she sigh'd, he hung his head.
Her lessening boat unwilling rows to land;
'Adieu!' she cries; and waved her lily hand.

HENRY CAREY

Sally In Our Alley

Of all the girls that are so smart
  There's none like pretty Sally;
She is the darling of my heart,
  And she lives in our alley.

There is no lady in the land
    Is half so sweet as Sally;
She is the darling of my heart,
    And she lives in our alley.

Her father he makes cabbage-nets
    And through the streets does cry 'em;
Her mother she sells laces long
    To such as please to buy 'em:
But sure such folks could ne'er beget
    So sweet a girl as Sally!
She is the darling of my heart,
    And she lives in our alley.

When she is by, I leave my work,
    I love her so sincerely;
My master comes like any Turk,
    And bangs me most severely —
But let him bang his bellyfull,
    I'll bear it all for Sally;
She is the darling of my heart,
    And she lives in our alley.

Of all the days that's in the week
    I dearly love but one day —
And that's the day that comes betwixt
    A Saturday and Monday;
For then I'm drest all in my best
    To walk abroad with Sally

She is the darling of my heart,
　　And she lives in our alley.

My master carries me to church,
　　And often am I blamed
Because I leave him in the lurch
　　As soon as text is named;
I leave the church in sermon-time
　　And slink away to Sally;
She is the darling of my heart,
　　And she lives in our alley.

When Christmas comes about again
　　O then I shall have money;
I'll hoard it up, and box it all,
　　I'll give it to my honey;
I would it were ten thousand pound,
　　I'd give it all to Sally;
She is the darling of my heart,
　　And she lives in our alley.

My master and the neighbours all
　　Make game of me and Sally,
And, but for her, I'd better be
　　A slave and row a galley;
But when my seven long years are out
　　O then I'll marry Sally, –
O then we'll wed, and then we'll bed,
　　But not in our alley!

Robert Burns

'Ye banks and braes o' bonnie Doon'

Ye banks and braes o' bonnie Doon,
　　How can ye blume sae fair!
How can ye chant, ye little birds,
　　And I sae fu' o' care!

Thou'll break my heart, thou bonnie bird
　　That sings upon the bough;
Thou minds me o' the happy days
　　When my fause Luve was true.

Thou'll break my heart, thou bonnie bird
　　That sings beside thy mate;
For sae I sat, and sae I sang,
　　And wist na o' my fate.

Aft hae I roved by bonnie Doon
　　To see the woodbine twine,
And ilka bird sang o' its love;
　　And sae did I o' mine.

Wi' lightsome heart I pu'd a rose,
　　Frae aff its thorny tree;
And my fause luver staw the rose,
　　But left the thorn wi' me.

ROBERT BURNS

'O my Luve's like a red, red rose'

O my Luve's like a red, red rose
   That's newly sprung in June:
O my Luve's like the melodie
   That's sweetly play'd in tune.

As fair art thou, my bonnie lass,
   So deep in luve am I:
And I will luve thee still, my dear,
   Till a' the seas gang dry:

Till a' the seas gang dry, my dear,
   And the rocks melt wi' the sun;
I will luve thee still, my dear,
   While the sands o' life shall run.

And fare thee weel, my only Luve!
   And fare thee weel awhile!
And I will come again, my Luve,
   Tho' it were ten thousand mile.

Robert Burns

John Anderson

John Anderson my jo, John,
When we were first acquent
Your locks were like the raven,
Your bonnie brow was brent;
But now your brow is bald, John,
Your locks are like the snow;
But blessings on your frosty pow,
John Anderson my jo.

John Anderson my jo, John,
We clamb the hill thegither,
And mony a canty day, John,
We've had wi' ane anither:
Now we maun totter down, John,
But hand in hand we'll go,
And sleep thegither at the foot,
John Anderson my jo.

Samuel Taylor Coleridge

Love

All thoughts, all passions, all delights,
Whatever stirs this mortal frame,

All are but ministers of Love,
    And feed his sacred flame.

Oft in my waking dreams do I
Live o'er again that happy hour,
When midway on the mount I lay,
    Beside the ruin'd tower.

The moonshine stealing o'er the scene
Had blended with the lights of eve;
And she was there, my hope, my joy,
    My own dear Genevieve!

She lean'd against the arméd man,
The statue of the arméd knight;
She stood and listen'd to my lay,
    Amid the lingering light.

Few sorrows hath she of her own,
My hope! my joy! my Genevieve!
She loves me best, whene'er I sing
    The songs that make her griev

I play'd a soft and doleful air,
I sang an old and moving story —
An old rude song, that suited well
    That ruin wild and hoary.

She listen'd with a flitting blush,
With downcast eyes and modest grace;
For well she knew, I could not choose
    But gaze upon her face.

I told her of the Knight that wore
Upon his shield a burning brand;
And that for ten long years he woo'd
    The Lady of the Land

I told her how he pined: and ah!
The deep, the low, the pleading tone
With which I sang another's love
    Intepreted my own.

She listen'd with a flitting blush,
With downcast eyes, and modest grace;
And she forgave me, that I gazed
    Too fondly on her face!

But when I told the cruel scorn
That crazed that bold and lovely Knight,
And that he cross'd the mountain-woods,
    Nor rested day nor night;

That sometimes from the savage den,
And sometimes from the darksome shade,
And sometimes starting up at once
    In green and sunny glade.

There came and look'd him in the face
An angel beautiful and bright;
And that he knew it was a Fiend,
    This miserable Knight!

And that unknowing what he did,
He leap'd amid a murderous band,
And saved from outrage worse than death
   The Lady of the Land;

And how she wept, and clasp'd his knees;
And how she tended him in vain;
And ever strove to expiate
   The scorn that crazed his brain;

And that she nursed him in a cave,
And how his madness went away,
When on the yellow forest-leaves
   A dying man he lay;

– His dying words – but when I reach'd
That tenderest strain of all the ditty,
My faltering voice and pausing harp
   Disturb'd her soul with pity!

All impulses of soul and sense
Had thrill'd my guileless Genevieve;
The music and the doleful tale,
   The rich and balmy eve;

And hopes, and fears that kindle hope,
An undistinguishable throng,
And gentle wishes long subdued,
   Subdued and cherish'd long!

She wept with pity and delight,
She blush'd with love, and virgin shame;
And like the murmur of a dream,
    I heard her breathe my name.

Her bosom heaved — she stepp'd aside,
As conscious of my look she stept —
Then suddenly, with timorous eye
    She fled to me and wept.

She half enclosed me with her arms,
She press'd me with a meek embrace;
And bending back her head, look'd up,
    And gazed upon my face.

'Twas partly love, and partly fear,
And partly 'twas a bashful art
That I might rather feel, than see,
    The swelling of her heart.

I calm'd her fears, and she was calm,
And told her love with virgin pride;
And so I won my Genevieve,
    My bright and beauteous Bride.

LORD BYRON

All For Love

O talk not to me of a name great in story;
The days of our youth are the days of our glory;
And the myrtle and ivy of sweet two-and-twenty
Are worth all your laurels though ever so plenty.

What are garlands and crowns to the brow that is
    wrinkled?
'Tis but as a dead flower with May-dew besprinkled:
Then away with all such from the head that is hoary —
What care I for the wreaths that can only give glory?

Oh Fame! — if I e'er took delight in thy praises,
'Twas less for the sake of thy high-sounding phrases,
Than to see the bright eyes of the dear one discover
She thought that I was not unworthy to love her.

There chiefly I sought thee, there only I found thee;
Her glance was the best of the rays that surround thee;
When it sparkled o'er aught that was bright in my
    story,
I knew it was love, and I felt it was glory.

Lord Byron

She walks in beauty, like the night

She walks in beauty, like the night
Of cloudless climes and starry skies,
And all that's best of dark and bright
Meet in her aspect and her eyes;
Thus mellow'd to that tender light
Which heaven to gaudy day denies.

One shade the more, one ray the less,
Had half impair'd the nameless grace
Which waves in every raven tress
Or softly lightens o'er her face,
Where thoughts serenely sweet express
How pure, how dear their dwelling-place.

And on that cheek and o'er the brow
So soft, so calm, yet eloquent,
The smiles that win, the tints that glow
But tell of days in goodness spent,
A mind at peace with all below,
A heart whose love is innocent.

LORD BYRON

When we two parted

When we two parted
In silence and tears,
Half broken-hearted,
To sever for years,
Pale grew thy cheek and cold,
Colder thy kiss;
Truly that hour foretold
Sorrow to this!

The dew of the morning
Sunk chill on my brow;
It felt like the warning
Of what I feel now.
Thy vows are all broken,
And light is thy fame:
I hear thy name spoken
And share in its shame.

They name thee before me,
A knell to mine ear;
A shudder comes o'er me –
Why wert thou so dear?
They know not I knew thee
Who knew thee too well:

Long, long shall I rue thee
Too deeply to tell.

In secret we met:
In silence I grieve
That thy heart could forget,
Thy spirit deceive.
If I should meet thee
After long years,
How should I greet thee? —
With silence and tears.

LORD BYRON

Elegy on Thyrza

And thou art dead, as young and fair
    As aught of mortal birth;
And forms so soft and charms so rare
    Too soon return'd to Earth!
Though Earth received them in her bed,
And o'er the spot the crowd may tread
    In carelessness or mirth,
There is an eye which could not brook
A moment on that grave to look.

I will not ask where thou liest low
    Nor gaze upon the spot;

There flowers or weeds at will may grow
    So I behold them not:
It is enough for me to prove
That what I loved, and long must love
Like common earth can rot;
To me there needs no stone to tell
'Tis Nothing that I loved so well.

Yet did I love thee to the last,
    As fervently as thou
Who didst not change through all the past
    And canst not alter now.
The love where Death has set his seal
Nor age can chill, nor rival steal,
    Nor falsehood disavow:
And, what were worse, thou canst not see
Or wrong, or change, or fault in me.

The better days of life were ours,
    The worst can be but mine:
The sun that cheers, the storm that lours,
    Shall never more be thine.
The silence of that dreamless sleep
I envy now too much to weep;
    Nor need I to repine
That all those charms have pass'd away
I might have watch'd through long decay.

The flower in ripen'd bloom unmatch'd
    Must fall the earliest prey;

Though by no hand untimely snatch'd,
  The leaves must drop away.
And yet it were a greater grief
To watch it withering, leaf by leaf,
  Than see it pluck'd to-day;
Since earthly eye but ill can bear
To trace the change to foul from fair.

I know not if I could have borne
  To see thy beauties fade;
The night that follow'd such a morn
  Had worn a deeper shade:
Thy day without a cloud hath past,
And thou wert lovely to the last,
  Extinguish'd, not decay'd;
As stars that shoot along the sky
Shine brightest as they fall from high.

As once I wept, if I could weep,
  My tears might well be shed
To think I was not near, to keep
  One vigil o'er thy bed:
To gaze, how fondly! on thy face,
To fold thee in a faint embrace,
  Uphold thy drooping head;
And show that love, however vain,
Nor thou nor I can feel again.

Yet how much less it were to gain,
  Though thou hast left me free,

The loveliest things that still remain
    Than thus remember thee!
The all of thine that cannot die
Through dark and dread Eternity
    Returns again to me,
And more thy buried love endears
Than aught except its living years.

WILLIAM WORDSWORTH

The Lost Love

She dwelt among the untrodden ways
    Beside the springs of Dove;
A maid whom there were none to praise,
    And very few to love.

A violet by a mossy stone
    Half-hidden from the eye!
– Fair as a star, when only one
    Is shining in the sky.

She lived unknown, and few could know
    When Lucy ceased to be;
But she is in her grave, and, O!
    The difference to me!

WILLIAM WORDSWORTH

Desideria

Surprized by joy – impatient as the wind –
I turn'd to share the transport – O with whom
But Thee – deep buried in the silent tomb,
That spot which no vicissitude can find?

Love, faithful love recall'd thee to my mind –
But how could I forget thee? Through what power
Even for the least division of an hour
Have I been so beguiled as to be blind

To my most grievous loss – That thought's return
Was the worst pang that sorrow ever bore
Save one, one only, when I stood forlorn,

Knowing my heart's best treasure was no more;
That neither present time, nor years unborn
Could to my sight that heavenly face restore.

THOMAS CAMPBELL

Freedom And Love

How delicious is the winning
Of a kiss at love's beginning,

When two mutual hearts are sighing
For the knot there's no untying!

Yet remember, 'midst your wooing
Love has bliss, but Love has ruing;
Other smiles may make you fickle,
Tears for other charms may trickle.

Love he comes and Love he tarries
Just as fate or fancy carries;
Longest stays, when sorest chidden;
Laughs and flies, when press'd and bidden.

Bind the sea to slumber stilly,
Bind its odour to the lily,
Bind the aspen ne'er to quiver,
Then bind Love to last for ever.

Love's a fire that needs renewal
Of fresh beauty for its fuel:
Love's wing moults when caged and captured,
Only free, he soars enraptured.

Can you keep the bee from ranging,
Or the ringdove's neck from changing?
No! nor fetter'd Love from dying
In the knot there's no untying.

PERCY BYSSHE SHELLEY

Love's Philosophy

The fountains mingle with the river
And the rivers with the ocean,
The winds of heaven mix for ever
With a sweet emotion;
Nothing in the world is single,
All things by a law divine
In one another's being mingle –
Why not I with thine?

See the mountains kiss high heaven
And the waves clasp one another;
No sister-flower would be forgiven
If it disdain'd its brother:
And the sunlight clasps the earth,
And the moonbeams kiss the sea –
What are all these kissings worth,
If thou kiss not me?

PERCY BYSSHE SHELLEY

The Flight Of Love

When the lamp is shatter'd
The light in the dust lies dead –

When the cloud is scatter'd,
The rainbow's glory is shed.
When the lute is broken,
Sweet tones are remember'd not;
When the lips have spoken,
Loved accents are soon forgot.

As music and splendour
Survive not the lamp and the lute,
The heart's echoes render
No song when the spirit is mute —
No song but sad dirges,
Like the wind through a ruin'd cell,
Or the mournful surges
That ring the dead seaman's knell.

When hearts have once mingled,
Love first leaves the well-built nest;
The weak one is singled
To endure what it once possesst.
O Love! who bewailest
The frailty of all things here,
Why choose you the frailest
For your cradle, your home, and your bier?

Its passions will rock thee
As the storms rock the ravens on high;
Bright reason will mock thee
Like the sun from a wintry sky.

From thy nest every rafter
Will rot, and thine eagle home
Leave thee naked to laughter,
When leaves fall and cold winds come.

Sir Walter Scott

Where Shall the Lover Rest

Where shall the lover rest
  Whom the fates sever
From his true maiden's breast,
  Parted for ever?
Where through groves deep and high
  Sounds the far billow,
Where early violets die
  Under the willow.
    Eleu loro
Soft shall be his pillow.

There, through the summer day
  Cool streams are laving:
There, while the tempests sway,
  Scarce are boughs waving;
There thy rest shalt thou take,
  Parted for ever,

Never again to wake,
    Never, O never!
        Eleu loro
    Never, O never!

Where shall the traitor rest,
    He, the deceiver,
Who could win maiden's breast,
    Ruin, and leave her?
In the lost battle,
    Borne down by the flying,
Where mingles war's rattle
    With groans of the dying;
        Eleu loro
    There shall he be lying.

Her wing shall the eagle flap
    O'er the falsehearted;
His warm blood the wolf shall lap
    Ere life be parted:
Shame and dishonour sit
    By his grave ever;
Blessing shall hallow it
    Never, O never!
        Eleu loro
    Never, O never!

SIR WALTER SCOTT

The Maid of Neidpath

O lovers' eyes are sharp to see,
    And lovers' ears in hearing;
And love, in life's extremity,
    Can lend an hour of cheering.
Disease had been in Mary's bower
    And slow decay from mourning,
Though now she sits on Neidpath's tower
    To watch her Love's returning.

All sunk and dim her eyes so bright,
    Her form decay'd by pining,
Till through her wasted hand, at night,
    You saw the taper shining.
By fits a sultry hectic hue
    Across her cheek was flying;
By fits so ashy pale she grew
    Her maidens thought her dying.

Yet keenest powers to see and hear
    Seem'd in her frame residing;
Before the watch-dog prick'd his ear
    She heard her lover's riding;
Ere scarce a distant form was kenn'd
    She knew and waved to greet him,
And o'er the battlement did bend

As on the wing to meet him.

He came – he pass'd – an heedless gaze
    As o'er some stranger glancing;
Her welcome, spoke in faltering phrase,
    Lost in his courser's prancing –
The castle-arch, whose hollow tone
    Returns each whisper spoken,
Could scarcely catch the feeble moan
    Which told her heart was broken.

JOHN KEATS

La Belle Dame Sans Merci

'O what can ail thee, knight-at-arms,
    Alone and palely loitering?
The sedge has wither'd from the lake,
    And no birds sing.

'O what can ail thee, knight-at-arms!
    So haggard and so woe-begone?
The squirrel's granary is full,
    And the harvest's done.

I see a lily on thy brow
    With anguish moist and fever-dew,
And on thy cheeks a fading rose

Fast withereth too.'

'I met a lady in the meads,
    Full beautiful – a faery's child,
Her hair was long, her foot was light,
    And her eyes were wild.

'I made a garland for her head,
    And bracelets too, and fragrant zone;
She look'd at me as she did love,
    And made sweet moan.

'I set her on my pacing steed
    And nothing else saw all day long,
For sidelong would she bend, and sing
    A fairy's song.

'She found me roots of relish sweet
    And honey wild and manna-dew,
And sure in language strange she said
    "I love thee true."

'She took me to her elfin grot,
    And there she wept and sigh'd full sore,
And there I shut her wild wild eyes
    With kisses four.

'And there she lullèd me asleep,
    And there I dream'd – Ah! woe betide!
The latest dream I ever dream'd
    On the cold hill's side.

'I saw pale kings and princes too,
    Pale warriors, death-pale were they all,
They cried – "La belle Dame sans Merci
    Hath thee in thrall!"

'I saw their starved lips in the gloam
    With horrid warning gapéd wide,
And I awoke and found me here
    On the cold hill's side.

'And this is why I sojourn here
    Alone and palely loitering,
Though the sedge is wither'd from the lake,
    And no birds sing.'

JAMES CLARENCE MANGAN

Dark Rosaleen

O my Dark Rosaleen,
    Do not sigh, do not weep!
The priests are on the ocean green,
    They march along the deep.
There's wine from the royal Pope,
    Upon the ocean green;
And Spanish ale shall give you hope,
    My Dark Rosaleen!
    My own Rosaleen!

Shall glad your heart, shall give you hope,
Shall give you health, and help, and hope,
　My Dark Rosaleen!

Over hills, and thro' dales,
　Have I roam'd for your sake;
All yesterday I sail'd with sails
　On river and on lake.
The Erne, at its highest flood,
　I dash'd across unseen.
For there was lightning in my blood,
　My Dark Rosaleen!
　My own Rosaleen!
O, there was lightning in my blood,
Red lightning lighten'd thro' my blood,
　My Dark Rosaleen!

All day long, in unrest,
　To and fro do I move.
The very soul within my breast
　Is wasted for you, love!
The heart in my bosom faints
　To think of you, my Queen,
My life of life, my saint of saints,
　My Dark Rosaleen!
　My own Rosaleen!
To hear your sweet and sad complaints,
My life, my love, my saint of saints,
　My Dark Rosaleen!

Woe and pain, pain and woe,
  Are my lot, night and noon,
To see your bright face clouded so,
  Like to the mournful moon.
But yet will I rear your throne
  Again in golden sheen;
'Tis you shall reign, shall reign alone,
  My Dark Rosaleen!
  My own Rosaleen!
'Tis you shall have the golden throne,
'Tis you shall reign, and reign alone,
  My dark Rosaleen!

Over dews, over sands,
  Will I fly, for your weal:
Your holy delicate white hands
  Shall girdle me with steel.
At home, in your emerald bowers,
  From morning's dawn till e'en,
You'll pray for me, my flower of flowers,
  My Dark Rosaleen!
  My fond Rosaleen!
You'll think of me thro' daylight hours,
My virgin flower, my flower of flowers,
  My Dark Rosaleen!

I could scale the blue air,
  I could plough the high hills,

O, I could kneel all night in prayer,
  To heal your many ills!
And one beamy smile from you
  Would float like light between
My toils and me, my own, my true,
  My Dark Rosaleen!
  My fond Rosaleen!
Would give me life and soul anew,
A second life, a soul anew,
  My Dark Rosaleen!

O, the Erne shall run red,
  With redundance of blood,
The earth shall rock beneath our tread,
  And flames wrap hill and wood,
And gun-peal and slogan-cry
  Wake many a glen serene,
Ere you shall fade, ere you shall die,
  My Dark Rosaleen!
  My own Rosaleen!
The Judgment Hour must first be nigh,
Ere you can fade, ere you can die,
  My Dark Rosaleen!

Sonnet From The Portuguese

When our two souls stand up erect and strong,
  Face to face, silent, drawing nigh and nigher,
  Until the lengthening wings break into fire
At either curving point, – what bitter wrong
Can the earth do us, that we should not long
  Be here contented! Think! In mounting higher,
  The angels would press on us, and aspire
To drop some golden orb of perfect song
Into our deep, dear silence. Let us stay
  Rather on earth, Belovéd – where the unfit
Contrarious moods of men recoil away
  And isolate pure spirits, and permit
A place to stand and love in for a day,
  With darkness and the death-hour rounding it.

The Ways of Love

How do I love thee? Let me count the ways.
I love thee to the depth and breadth and height
My soul can reach, when feeling out of sight
For the ends of Being and ideal Grace.

I love thee to the level of every day's
Most quiet need, by sun and candlelight.
I love thee freely, as men strive for Right:
I love thee purely, as they turn from Praise.

I love thee with the passion put to use
In my old griefs, and with my childhood's faith.
I love thee with a love I seemed to lose
With my lost saints, – I love thee with the breath,
Smiles, tears, of all my life! – and, if God choose,
I shall be love thee better after death.

LORD TENNYSON

The Lady of Shalott

PART I

On either side the river lie
Long fields of barley and of rye,
That clothe the wold and meet the sky;
And thro' the field the road runs by
         To many-tower'd Camelot;
And up and down the people go,
Gazing where the lilies blow
Round an island there below,
         The island of Shalott.

Willows whiten, aspens quiver,
Little breezes dusk and shiver

Thro' the wave that runs for ever
By the island in the river
              Flowing down to Camelot.
Four gray walls, and four gray towers,
Overlook a space of flowers,
And the silent isle imbowers
              The Lady of Shalott.

By the margin, willow-veil'd,
Slide the heavy barges trail'd
By slow horses; and unhail'd
The shallop flitteth silken-sail'd
              Skimming down to Camelot:
But who hath seen her wave her hand?
Or at the casement seen her stand?
Or is she known in all the land,
              The Lady of Shalott?

Only reapers, reaping early
In among the bearded barley,
Hear a song that echoes cheerly
From the river winding clearly,
              Down to tower'd Camelot:
And by the moon the reaper weary,
Piling sheaves in uplands airy,
Listening, whispers, ''Tis the fairy
              Lady of Shalott.'

PART II

There she weaves by night and day
A magic web with colours gay.
She has heard a whisper say,
A curse is on her if she stay
        To look down to Camelot.
She knows not what the curse may be,
And so she weaveth steadily,
And little other care hath she,
        The Lady of Shalott.

And moving thro' a mirror clear
That hangs before her all the year,
Shadows of the world appear.
There she sees the highway near
        Winding down to Camelot:
There the river eddy whirls,
And there the surly village-churls,
And the red cloaks of market girls,
        Pass onward from Shalott.

Sometimes a troop of damsels glad,
An abbot on an ambling pad,
Sometimes a curly shepherd-lad,
Or long-hair'd page in crimson clad,
        Goes by to tower'd Camelot;
And sometimes thro' the mirror blue
The knights come riding two and two:

She hath no loyal knight and true,
        The Lady of Shalott.

But in her web she still delights
To weave the mirror's magic sights,
For often thro' the silent nights
A funeral, with plumes and lights,
        And music, went to Camelot:
Or when the moon was overhead,
Came two young lovers lately wed;
'I am half-sick of shadows,' said
        The Lady of Shalott.

PART III

A bow-shot from her bower-eaves,
He rode between the barley-sheaves,
The sun came dazzling thro' the leaves,
And flamed upon the brazen greaves,
        Of bold Sir Lancelot.
A red-cross knight for ever kneel'd
To a lady in his shield,
That sparkled on the yellow field,
        Beside remote Shalott.

The gemmy bridle glitter'd free,
Like to some branch of stars we see
Hung in the golden Galaxy.

The bridle bells rang merrily
            As he rode down to Camelot:
And from his blazon'd baldric slung
A mighty silver bugle hung,
And as he rode his armour rung,
            Beside remote Shalott.

All in the blue unclouded weather
Thick-jewell'd shone the saddle-leather,
The helmet and the helmet-feather
Burn'd like one burning flame together,
            As he rode down to Camelot.
As often thro' the purple night,
Below the starry clusters bright,
Some bearded meteor, trailing light,
            Moves over still Shalott.

His broad clear brow in sunlight glow'd,
On burnish'd hooves his war-horse trode;
From underneath his helmet flow'd
His coal-black curls as on he rode,
            As he rode down to Camelot.
From the bank and from the river
He flash'd into the crystal mirror,
'Tirra lirra,' by the river
            Sang Sir Lancelot.

She left the web, she left the loom,
She made three paces thro' the room,

She saw the water-lily bloom,
She saw the helmet and the plume,
        She look'd down to Camelot.
Out flew the web and floated wide;
The mirror crack'd from side to side;
'The curse is come upon me,' cried
        The Lady of Shalott.

PART IV

In the stormy east-wind straining,
The pale yellow woods were waning,
The broad stream in his banks complaining,
Heavily the low sky raining
        Over tower'd Camelot;
Down she came and found a boat
Beneath a willow left afloat,
And round about the prow she wrote
        The Lady of Shalott.

And down the river's dim expanse –
Like some bold seer in a trance,
Seeing all his own mischance –
With a glassy countenance
        Did she look to Camelot.
And at the closing of the day
She loosed the chain, and down she lay;

The broad stream bore her far away,
        The Lady of Shalott.

Lying, robed in snowy white
That loosely flew to left and right —
The leaves upon her falling light —
Thro' the noises of the night
        She floated down to Camelot:
And as the boat-head wound along
The willowy hills and fields among,
They heard her singing her last song,
        The Lady of Shalott.

Heard a carol, mournful, holy,
Chanted loudly, chanted lowly,
Till her blood was frozen slowly,
And her eyes were darken'd wholly,
        Turn'd to tower'd Camelot.
For ere she reach'd upon the tide
The first house by the water-side,
Singing in her song she died,
        The Lady of Shalott.

Under tower and balcony,
By garden-wall and gallery,
A gleaming shape she floated by,
Dead-pale between the houses high,
        Silent into Camelot.
Out upon the wharfs they came

Knight and burgher, lord and dame,
And round the prow they read her name,
      The Lady of Shalott.

Who is this? and what is here?
And in the lighted palace near
Died the sound of royal cheer;
And they cross'd themselves for fear,
      All the knights at Camelot:
But Lancelot mused a little space;
He said, 'She has a lovely face;
God in his mercy lend her grace,
      The Lady of Shalott.'

EMILY BRONTË

Remembrance

Cold in the earth – and the deep snow piled above thee,
Far, far, removed, cold in the dreary grave!
Have I forgot, my only Love, to love thee,
Severed at last by Time's all-severing wave?

Now, when alone, do my thoughts no longer hover
Over the mountains, on that northern shore,
Resting their wings where heath and fern-leaves cover
Thy noble heart for ever, ever more?

Cold in the earth – and fifteen wild Decembers,
From those brown hills, have melted into spring:
Faithful, indeed, is the spirit that remembers
After such years of change and suffering!

Sweet Love of youth, forgive, if I forget thee,
While the world's tide is bearing me along;
Other desires and other hopes beset me,
Hopes which obscure, but cannot do thee wrong!

No later light has lightened up my heaven,
No second morn has ever shone for me;
All my life's bliss from thy dear life was given,
All my life's bliss is in the grave with thee.

But, when the days of golden dreams had perished,
And even Despair was powerless to destroy;
Then did I learn how existence could be cherished,
Strengthened and fed without the aid of joy.

Then did I check the tears of useless passion –
Weaned my young soul from yearning after thine;
Sternly denied its burning wish to hasten
Down to that tomb already more than mine.

And, even yet, I dare not let it languish,
Dare not indulge in memory's rapturous pain;
Once drinking deep of that divinest anguish,
How could I seek the empty world again?

DANTE GABRIEL ROSSETTI

Silent Noon

Your hands lie open in the long fresh grass, –
   The finger-points look through like rosy blooms:
   Your eyes smile peace. The pasture gleams and
      glooms
'Neath billowing skies that scatter and amass.
All round our nest, far as the eye can pass,
   Are golden kingcup-fields with silver edge
   Where the cow-parsley skirts the hawthorn-hedge.
'Tis visible silence, still as the hour-glass.

Deep in the sun-searched growths the dragon-fly
Hangs like a blue thread loosened from the sky:–
   So this wing'd hour is dropt to us from above.
Oh! clasp we to our hearts, for deathless dower,
This close-companioned inarticulate hour
   When twofold silence was the song of love.

W. B. Yeats

'When you are old and gray and full of sleep'

When you are old and gray and full of sleep,
    And nodding by the fire, take down this book,
    And slowly read, and dream of the soft look
Your eyes had once, and of their shadows deep;

How many loved your moments of glad grace,
    And loved your beauty with love false or true;
    But one man loved the pilgrim soul in you,
And loved the sorrows of your changing face.

And bending down beside the glowing bars
    Murmur, a little sadly, how love fled
    And paced upon the mountains overhead,
And hid his face amid a crowd of stars.

W. B. YEATS

Down By The Salley Gardens

Down by the salley gardens my love and I did meet;
She passed the salley gardens with little snow-white
    feet.
She bid me take love easy, as the leaves grow on the
    tree;
But I, being young and foolish, with her would not
    agree.

In a field by the river my love and I did stand,
And on my leaning shoulder she laid her snow-white
    hand
She bid me take life easy, as the grass grows on the
    weirs;
But I was young and foolish, and now am full of tears.